Moment's We Couldn't Speak

Hardships of Teenage

AMAN

Published by Aman

First Edition

Cover Design by: Aman and Amit

This book is intended for informational and educational purposes only. The content reflects the author's personal experiences, research, and perspectives. While every effort has been made to ensure accuracy, readers should consult relevant professionals for specific advice or guidance. The author assumes no responsibility for any actions taken based on the contents of this book.

For permissions, inquiries, or other information, please contact:
aman.chaudhary9210@gmail.com

"To all those who are
fighting with themselves"

Contents

INTRODUCTION

I have always enjoyed writing, from participating in school competitions to delivering speeches in front of audience. For me, writing is not merely about presenting raw data; it is a way to connect with people of all kinds. It creates connections that can change their thinking and provide support. There are many topics we don't discuss openly, either because we feel ashamed or because those around us make us feel nervous. This creates a gap between us all. If we are not confident in our own thoughts, it is truly shameful. It doesn't matter if you are right or wrong; what matters is that you raise your voice and express yourself.

This call to action is not only for girls, who are often portrayed as weak and submissive, but also for the gentlemen who may lack the courage to speak up when they see something wrong. We have bound ourselves in the name of personal matters, neglecting our surroundings. Yet, we are often the ones who complain about societal discrimination and a lack of civic education. Until you take a step forward to be a good member of society, you will continue to live in a world where discrimination, racism, and a lack of civic sense are common issues.

I never considered writing a self-help book, nor did I think about writing a book at all. However, after navigating my teenage journey and experiencing unpredictable moments, I sought help. I searched online and in books, hoping to find reassurance that I was not alone in facing teenage hardships. I discovered that there were 1.3 billion others like me going through similar dark days, but to be honest, I found little help. The only option left was to wait—wait for time to heal me, and it did. After enduring those days of internal conflict and learning from my mistakes, I decided to write this book, which is now in your hands.

This book not only shares my experiences but also conveys the struggles, emotions, and joys of those precious moments that we all encounter in our lives. From the excitement of birth to the journey of getting to school, living alongside strangers for years, making friends, and cherishing the memories we create together, it all shapes who we are. As we move forward, we experience love and affection, which sometimes do not turn out well, leading us to struggle with trust again. We face numerous challenges but often remain silent, crying at night, regretting our decisions, and criticizing ourselves for every small failure. We feel burdened by the expectations of society, parents, friends, and our own aspirations. This can lead us into a deep silence where we struggle to see anything else. It takes time and effort to emerge from that silence, but once you do, you discover a stronger and better version of yourself.

I have found peace in being alone. I enjoy solitude because it provides me with a comfortable space to focus on myself rather than entertain a crowd. While I was not always inclined to be alone, time has taught me that those who live independently and are not surrounded by a multitude of people often lead more peaceful lives. I have a few close friends, who are enough for me to share my day with and seek help when needed.

I encourage my readers to accept themselves as they are. There is no need to change yourself to fit someone else's expectations. What truly matters is your personality and confidence in yourself. Every person is unique, and that uniqueness is your identity. If you choose to change yourself for any specific reason, be prepared to feel lost among the crowd.

Furthermore, this book will explore why you should not have expectations from others. Having expectations can become a burden. If someone fails to meet your expectations, you may feel disappointed; if they do meet them, you may become greedy and start dreaming, only to have those dreams shattered later. No one is free or understanding enough to dive into your mind and read your thoughts to fulfil your wishes. If you want something, work for it and earn it; then you will truly appreciate its worth.

Let us now explore and dive into the thoughts we often struggle to articulate. Let's spark this journey of memories and lessons, shall we?

Chapter 1

Here You Are: A Journey of Growth

Everyone shares the same beginning in life. We are all born, and we all cry for the first time. That cry marks the start of a new life, a unique entity brought into this world for a special purpose. The new flower, nurtured for nine months, whether unconditionally or conditionally, is finally here. Now, I can breathe in this miraculous world, filled with extraordinary things, people, and experiences.

My fists are tightly closed, my eyes are shut, and my heart beats fast. I am a novice in this world, ready to learn and accomplish so much. The journey ahead will surely not be easy; it is filled with obstacles we must confront and overcome. In the end, we must prove our existence: "Yes, I am here. I was born here, and I am living here."

I, Aman, am a part of this world, just like all of you. I take the initiative to share some beautiful as well as challenging moments I have experienced over my 19 years (as of 2024).

It is said that everyone is different; we each have our own cultures, traditions, beliefs, and values. However, I believe we all go through the same story of life—a story filled with excitement, joy, happiness, sadness, stress, worry, struggle, and more. This cycle is what connects us all. What truly matters is what we choose, how we work toward our goals, and what we ultimately achieve.

So, let's embark on this journey together and explore whether it's true that we are all the same or if we are indeed far apart.

Shall we?

I was born and raised in a middle-class
family. Before me, my elder sister had already
taken her place, making our family complete.
I have a loving mom, a hard-working dad, and
an occasionally annoying sister. The days I
remember were beautiful because, as children,
we possessed an innate curiosity about
everything. We are like new players in this
world, eager to explore and learn about
everything with great enthusiasm.

We find joy in even the smallest things, such
as tiny creatures like ants. I vividly remember
how we used to gaze at them for long periods,
often for no particular reason. We broke many
things, dropped countless items, playfully
kicked our cousins, and cried whenever we
felt hungry or unsafe. This period is the most
beautiful time in a person's life because
everything is unconditional. The word
unconditional carries a profound meaning,
and I know that readers understand it well.

As we grow, we do so slowly and step by
step. With every new step, we learn
something valuable and move forward. Little

by little, those tiny crawling feet begin to stand on their own. Bravo! You did it! The first moment that excites your family is when they realize their child is trying. Then, with a gentle push, you start to run like a racing car—full of energy, with no direction or brakes—until you eventually come to a dramatic stop: BOOM.

Yes, I admit that I broke a lot of things when I was a kid, including myself. We all experience some form of hurt at that age, and during those formative years, our families nurture us with intense care.

Slowly, we become ready to step into this world. The first step you are about to take is—guess what? Yes, you guessed it right: school. It's an experience we might hate now, or perhaps one we will miss later. So, let's embark on this journey to school together.

?.

Chapter 2

Let's Get into It

Everything in this world follows a particular process in which there are multiple stages. Just think of a butterfly and how it takes birth—from the egg to caterpillar to pupa, and finally to one of the most beautiful creatures on this earth: the butterfly. The beautiful art woven by nature on the wings of a butterfly takes time. It's not done just in a day. **Remember, beautiful things take time to fly.** You are as beautiful as a butterfly, born and raised here, and will fly high in the future.

Let's continue the beautiful journey from the leaves to the sky. Are you ready?

Last time, we discussed how a magic trick happens in this world when you are born. After spending 2 or 3 years with your family, it's time to take the first step into society.

Remember those days—new school bag, new shoes, new books, and everything. It was just like Christmas for us. We were all so excited and happy to get all those things! The first day of school, when your mom drops you off at the school bus, and the first time you travel with people and kids who are complete strangers. You gaze outside the window and notice many things, which make you both excited and confused. Then you arrive at school, and your teacher takes you all the way to your seat. I always notice that those little ones are very quiet because they don't know what's going on. For them, it's all very new, and they are still trying to understand everything. You learn how to speak, how to write your own name, and what more you can do!

Did you know that when a kid cries, and you give them candy, they stop? Ever wondered why? The reason is simple—when you offer candy, all their attention shifts from the pain to the candy. The child remembers that they love it and get used to eating it. Instead of crying, the kid focuses on that delicious candy. Kids are said to have the purest form of human nature because they haven't learned anything else yet. For them, everything is the same—no black, no white, no religion, no caste, nothing. And that's how you make friends in your school time. You talk to people like you, get involved with them, and make a connection with them, and you name it "friendship." Little by little, it gets deeper, and you become best friends.

At that time, one person holds a special place in your heart that may or may not be occupied by someone else. You play together, spend great time together with that friend, and take your friendship a long way. You grow together, learn together, experience together, fail together, and rise together. That period of time takes you up to 9th grade. During that time, you study and learn new things. Taking part in school events has always been exciting and fun, hasn't it? I took part in all the events organized by my school because that's where you learn something new from your bunch of books and meet new people.

Then you slowly start to move to the teenage phase of your life. The most crucial phase, where you face so many things you could never even dream of. Do you like watching movies? How would it be if your life became like a movie on a rollercoaster? I'm sure you all know about a rollercoaster ride. Let me take you on one now..

؟

Chapter 3

Blooming Through Changes: The Teenage Experience

Guys, you know what? I have loved doing gardening in my free time, and I still do it. The beautiful little plants with green leaves and a beautiful bloom. I am sure that there will not be any person who will hate trees; we all love them because we know their importance in our lives. From food to wood and air we breath, shed, temperature regulation, and even the beautiful calligraphy that we all praise, shedding leaves in the autumn season. The autumn festival shows us the flow of life to death and regeneration. Old leaves shed and new ones come.

Have you all noticed that new one, the very small tree that just came out of the ground? The seed germination is a long process, but when finally, that small plant from that seed comes out, it needs very much care and attention. The seed germination is a long process, but when finally, that small plant from that seed comes out, it needs very much care and attention. We are just like that small tree in our teenage years.

That small plant experiences sunshine for the first time and finds a massive world around it, in which there are humans, animals, and sky-touching trees. We all as well experience the depth of our lives in our teen years. We enter a society, understand its ethics, and develop our own opinion. It can be supportive or contradictory to it, which doesn't matter. You have got a brain in your head, which you use differently from other people.

I think that most of the readers who are reading this book might have already passed their teenage years or might be in their teens. For all of those, I appreciate that you all are fighting and keep going with it. I deeply understand how things might be going with you, but I believe and have faith in you that you can do it.

In the upcoming chapters, we will be discussing various stages and problems that we all face in our teen years, but we never share them with anyone because we feel that's just something with us, and others may laugh if you share your personal things with them. Well, that's how I was too. I never shared my things with anyone because I felt that there would not be any solution for them, and I had to keep going with them. But now, I am writing and discussing all of them here with you all so that you don't feel alone.

Teenage Quest

Most people experience their teenage or adolescent years in their 13–19 years of age in their life. We can divide this as 13-15 is considered an early teen, 16-17 is termed a middle teen, and 18-19 is known as a late teen. This age can differ by various factors, like the environment around a person, friends, society, and cultural influence. Some can experience early adolescence, and some may experience it later.

In the time period of a teenager, a person experiences various physical and mental changes in his/her body and mind. From height to skin, from body hair to voice change, and mentally we experience truly various changes like sexual development, emotional change, relationships, identity identification, our own opinion, conflicts with society, family, friends' breakdowns, and what else.

In this chapter we will discuss the physical charges, and further we go through the mental ones because I know they have a lot to explain and motivate.

Plugging into Transformation

At the age of puberty, boys and girls experience different physical changes. For boys, like facial hair growth increasing, we get beards and moustaches, muscles also grow and develop. There is a rapid increase in height, and that's why some get names like 'Mount Everest' or 'Pole.' And then you were used to changing the bulbs in your house and classrooms. And that pole was also threatening the small-height boys, who we used to nickname as 'chotte(Mr. Dwarf). Just think, you are walking in the hallway of your school and suddenly hear "Chotte, idhar ana" ("Hey! Shorty, come here! That time you wait for the blast of the ground and melt in it. Lol! Because you feel ashamed at that time, what more do you expect at that time?

But it was actually common; most people may take it lightly and ignore it, but some may not ignore it. Because there are three types of people: introverts, extroverts, and ambiverts. Let's discuss this briefly.

Two Worlds, One Balance: Introverts and Extroverts

Talking about introverts is far more difficult and hard because of what an introvert can feel you can never. And I feel that the extroverted person also used to be an introvert at some point, but the people around and situation made him come out like that.

Just imagine the same situation when you are walking in your school hall and someone pokes you with a funny nickname, and you are surrounded by a bunch of people who hear it. At that time the person can take two actions; either one will just take off his shoe and hit the one who said it. Which I consider is a better option because he ended up the matter there and did not take it over, but some just leave that site after being called like that. They feel the harm of self-respect within them and among other students, which is extremely common. This option is far worse because it stores guilt in your mind for life long that you lost your self-respect among other students' by being called by that funny name.

So please, I request to all those naughty friends that you can make fun and joke around with each other, and it is completely right. But the situation and place really matter. **"Making fun among 2 people and 200 people is very different"**. And always try not to harm the self-esteem of people around you because you don't know how it may affect their mental health.

An ambivert is one who is capable of maintaining his inner and outer behavior very well among others. Mean the one who can balance the introvert and extrovert traits well. Being honest, being an ambivert is not easy because they have to change themselves and their behavior as per the people around them. Sometimes they may lie to you as well because they want things to keep on going smoothly, but the reality is far from that. An ambivert can speak in a crowd of 1000, but still there may be a person who might be his lover or his family, where he hardly bears to speak about something.

Girls and Their Challenges

Let's now talk about the physical changes that the girl experiences at the age of puberty. Although I am not a girl, but, I have studied about it as well and asked my female friends as well. There are many things that boys and girls experience the same at puberty, like an increase in height and weight, body hair, muscle development, the onset of puberty (secretion of sexual hormones), etc. But some changes that only affect girls are breast development, body shape change, menstruation, vaginal discharge, and mood swings.

 Girls experience more tough times than boys when they hit puberty due to physical factors as well as periods. Periods are the time period for every girl where she goes through a lot of pain, which she even finds hard to tell someone. The pain in the first period is truly awful, and in periods girls majorly behave a little unusually because their minds swing at any time because of the pain they have been feeling inside them, and worse is that they cannot tell this clearly and openly to someone.

 I still remember when my female friend told me how hard it was for her when she got her periods, and she was crying when she was telling about this for the first time to her mom. Not only periods, but there are more things that are common for girls between them that they don't let out, mainly the discrimination that they face because of the changes they get in their skin color, the change in the geometry of their faces, their looks, and also their dressing style. These things may appear contradictory to and put a negative impression on others. And making a difference on such facial and body structure is surely wrong, no doubt. But this happen so lightly and softly and give a very silent agony inside the person's heart and mind.

Also, mostly in rural areas and places where the society and family are not much educated at those places, girls have to follow various rules and society's ethics. They have to think before wearing any kind of dress and applying something to their skin because they know that if they try to do something different than usual, they will get pointed at first by their family and then be peeked at and noticed by other people outside. In such situations, it is not the fault of society or the young girl.

Society is not just made by a person; when many people and groups of people meet and share their ideas of living, a lifestyle. and make rules and regulations, it is termed society. And these rules and regulations can be old and have not been modified.

So, people may find. something unusual and new when they see a girl wearing a skirt rather than a saree. Because they have mostly seen their women around in public at home in sarees, things like skirts and jeans may be new and can start a contradiction of thought. And neither the young girl is wrong, because in today's generation everyone has their own choice about dressing and decorating ourselves.

Also, the western and eastern dressing styles have influenced the people towards them. They like it because they are getting unique and new clothes that are far different from what they used to wear, so they also get a desire to wear them and feel that they are also part of the updated generation with time.

So just think about what could be the best solution in such a situation because both are right. Just try to think and figure it out. I'm sure either boy or girl who is reading it here may have gone through it at some point when your parents or other people stopped you or asked you not to wear something that you found cool. What do you think can be the best solution there? Well, the answer is quite easy, and just in 2 words, "understanding" and "acceptance.".

2 life principles: "Acceptance" and "Understanding"

These two principles may appear very easy to read, and most of us feel that we acquire both of them. But wait, dear, **NO ONE IS PERFECT HERE**; there have been various situations and real-life experiences where you have lacked these two rules, or maybe in the future you will. And it happens with us, but we barely notice it or we just ignore it. Let's take the same situation as before and handle it. What do you think? What would be your first step? Let's see..... Make your parents' and the people who find it not acceptable. Tell them that you are not the only one who is wearing them, but a lot more like you do wear, and to match and not get neglected from them, you have to wear.

And also try to explain how you find them different from what you originally wore and want to try them out. **NEVER EVER MAKE**

YOUR TONE LOUD OR BE RUDE IN THIS UNDERSTANDING PROCESS. **"Calmness is the ultimate way to reach success."**. This is the totally wrong way to raise your voice directly and reply rudely when someone points you out. If you do this, then you are making your own value down. That person pointed you out because he/she found it unusual, so it's your responsibility to give a clear justification and make that person understand. And if they don't, because some are very tightly bonded by their ethics, you can just ignore them. This will be your best approach to it. Learn how to deal with things calmly and wisely.

Now here is one question that can come into some brains: "**Why do I have to justify myself?** It's my choice to wear what I want, so why do I explain this to someone else?" Let's understand this with my own real-life example.

I will be honest and say that I love to wear western and eastern (mostly Korean and Japanese) outfits. I find them more suitable for me and really love them. Once there was a party, and I wore the baggy jeans with an open shirt and jacket over it and some accessories; that's how you mostly see your K-pop idol's right. So, I also made my hair and got there. Many of the people gathered there were wearing Indian traditional outfits, and I was the very one who wore such stylish and fashionable clothes. My friends were there, and we were all talking and having fun. But then an old man and other people who were hearing me asked me about my outfit: Why did I wear something like this?

Look, here is a catch. I could have chosen any one option among two options. Either I have told them very politely, or I have answered them rudely.

If I answered him very softly and politely, it would create a sense of understanding between the person I was talking with. I will explain that I love such clothes and find them more suitable for me. This approach shows my confidence, positive attitude, respect, open-minded behavior, and control over situations. The one who questioned me will be happy to know about my dressing sense and will understand it; if they still do not understand, then they will be silent because your calmness has previously suppressed the conflicting and negative thoughts in that person's mind, and no word can make him/her win that conversation because you already won it. **"Act like a sea and let your words and personality make a tsunami"**. Remember that calmness and word limit are important and the most powerful tools that you have by which you can win any battle. So, try it and live a life with confidence in yourself.

Now let's understand the concept of acceptance, which is quite easy if you read it logically with your brain cells open, okay? Let's take the same situation that we discussed before: that you found something not really appropriate for you. And you reach out to that person and ask him about that.

Reminder: You are a human, so behave like a human. Don't pounce on people like a lion. You have vocals, language, and brains, so use them and behave calmly. OK. I have seen people who come and ask like they are the smartest people, and what they say is right and all else is wrong. So please don't do that because, babe, it doesn't sound cool at all. Even the other person will think that you are such a stupid idiot who came from nowhere.

So, the tone and the softness that you maintain in your words is very necessary. Because you have a different opinion and you want to understand something new from another person, remember to be respectful and kind. And you shall always give a space to that person, which means, hear to him/her with a clear mind. Don't compare your thoughts because we are all the wisest personas in ourselves. We all think that no one is smarter than we are, and we all prioritize our thoughts first because, for us, they are the supreme and ultimate truth, which is wrong. Remember that no one can get all the knowledge of this universe in one brain.

There are 8 billion people on this planet, which gives rise to more than 80 billion thoughts that are very different from each other, and if you start to fight over them, how many more world wars will happen? No one will know. When you reach out to someone or anywhere, you are getting to learn something new, which is different from your own opinion. Listen to it and analyze it; find facts in it, compare your opinion and the opinion of another person, and find which one is more practical and impactful, and if the other one is right, press the update button of your software and update your data.

So far now, we have gotten to know about the physical and some general personal and society issues that we may face and also discussed a wise way to solve them. Further, we will dive into a deep sea of emotional and mental problems and circumstances we all go through, and let's analyze all of them. Don't be shy because "**you are not alone.**" So, let's move ahead with the same strength and energy, shall we!?

?

Chapter 4

Mental Health at Puberty

So far we all have got to know about the physical changes that we experience in our teenage years. Physical charges can vary from boy to girl. But here, we are going to discuss those changes that are mostly common in all genders. These all are the mental and emotional changes we will be discussing . We will try to figure out common challenges and how to conquer them. So, what are we waiting for? Let's get started.!

A scientific overview

I am also a science student. I personally believe a lot in science, so let's first get to know what and why we experience things, and then let's discuss things briefly.

During our teen years, or puberty, our brain goes under various changes, like prefrontal cortex development, which is responsible for the decision-making ability of a person. Do you know why teenagers love to do thrills, take risks, and get new experiences? It's because of the dopamine system, which influences the feelings of excitement and reward. Ever wondered why teenagers are so sensitive and take things seriously? It's because of the amygdala, which is responsible for fear and comfort. There are so many more changes that occur in our brain, and by then we start building ourselves into a new version of ourselves. I always say to all that after teenage, you get a new birth. Your life starts again, and you get ready to fly high.

Cage of darkness with light

You might have noticed that teenagers have mood swings a lot. Sometimes they are so happy that they have got all the joy of the world, but also it happens when we see them sitting in a deep silence consumed with thoughts. Why does it happen, and why do we experience it? Well - Well, at your puberty. We try to find a reason for everything; we want to know what is it. Why is it? And a lot more.

We all have studied the three states of matter: solid, liquid, and gas. Think of solid. The atoms in solids are so tightly packed with each other that there is not any movement. The same happens with us. As we take every shit in our mind and we question it. As we take every shit in our mind and we question it. Also, we think a lot and want to know the reason for things that are happening with us. These questions and thoughts all strike with each other and take you to silence, where you are completely blank and don't know anything.

It also happened with me. I also used to think a lot and wanted to find answers to my questions for hours. And at the end I just come out with a clean chit. Because I forced my brain to work a lot, it can't think and work anymore. You are a human, and you need rest to resolve things, so please don't let every stupid thing get into your brain, and then you come out as bare land. **"Plant only beautiful**

so that you have a beautiful garden ahead.".

Find yourself

"What you acknowledge yourself is more valuable than what you learn from others."

We all want to be independent and do whatever we want to. Either it is travelling across the globe, eating different food, exploring new places, having fun, spending time with family, and also many want to have a very beautiful and romantic life. Sorry, not many I say mostly, because there are also those who love Mafia love and dark love. No need for an explanation! Explore it yourself! We get so many different ideas and want to do them all at the moment or maybe in the future, and for that we want to be independent. No doubt travelling with family is fun, but travelling alone or with friends or with your loved ones gives you more unforgettable memories.

We want to be independent and explore everything. Want to learn new things, develop our own understanding, conclude things by ourselves, make decisions, and understand the real values of love and friends. But many are not able to because of various reasons, either family, financial, or personal reasons. And, it goes on like this. And it's not a problem with it because not everyone's condition is the same. Just want to tell you that you shouldn't blame anyone for what you are. Human is that organism whose desires and greed will never end. Work hard with whatever you have to get what you want. Have control over yourself and make a goal to achieve it.

Many of us want to be independent. Living alone and doing other stuff, but the first thing that sticks is within themselves. Will I be able to make it?

We are afraid of our own thoughts and desires to accomplish. We start questioning ourselves, like, what if I fail to do so? What if I do not get what I want and so much-- And you know what's the funniest thing here? It is that they make an imagination, and after 5 minutes they start questioning, and in another 2 minutes that goal is gone and a new one starts to get into you. And it keeps on going.

It's exactly like a song: when you listen to a band, you want to be a rockstar; when you hear a soft song, you want to be a singer; watching an action movie makes you want to be an actor; and when watching a vlog, you want to be a vlogger.

I want to say that. Stop! It is so much of you that you can't even focus on one thing. I know it's very normal, and we all go through this. But let me take you to the reality that if you keep on dreaming like this all the time without focusing on any one thing, then you will be destroyed.

Try different things and pick up what you like the most, and then start working on it and get a master so no one can beat you.

Being independent doesn't mean that you will just borrow money from your parents and enjoy. No

The meaning of being independent is to earn yourself and then spend on whatever or wherever the hell you want to, so you can explore the reality of life.

Sexual Identification and Attraction

This is the time when you explore yourself about what you are originally. But why did I mention sexual identification? Well, the reason is pretty simple but also hard to accept to some people as well; we all have heard about LGBTQIA+ people. But the thing is we don't really want to know about them and understand them because we feel that they are different from us, and sometimes we also regard them as unnatural (mostly people have kind of this opinion). But on a very simple note, they are human, and you are also a human. Just their preference is different and nothing more.

At puberty the sexual hormones segregate, and we start to have sexual desires and get attracted to others. It can either be a boy or a girl.

This attraction is the result of testosterone (in males) and estrogen (in females) and oxytocin (the love hormone), which makes one attracted to the other. We get more open to others' and start caring about ourselves more. We want to attract people and let them acknowledge us and praise us, and also we get a very hardcore desire to get a lover. I will discuss this in depth in upcoming chapters.

Loneliness and Depression

"There is an empty space within ourselves that no one can fill."

Some of us are lucky enough to not have to face these two terms at puberty, but everyone goes through it once in their life at least. This number can also increase depending on your environment and yourself. Loneliness is not about when you are not surrounded by people or having fun. It is actually a loss of yourself. And this is what can lead to depression further. Actually, depression is a far more painful period that can be given by you to yourself or others. You give them so much importance that when they leave you, you are just like a corpse.

If you start loving yourself and enjoying your own company, then you will really be very happy, but if you just focus on the empty space within yourself, then, sorry to say, life and living will be very hard for you.

Chapter 5

Friendship : A Flower with Thorns

One of the most beautiful relationships that we all have. This relation is one that lasts a lifetime. Not importantly with just one person but with many. Friendship is defined as that which is supportive and punishable too. And we all know why it is punishable, right?

But there is something that changes; wonder what? From your young age to your teen years, like from 9 to 13 or 13 to 15. There is a change in the friendship boundaries, the boundations, and their depth. Here we are going to discuss them.

So, without wasting our time, let's get started!

Conflicts and Harmony

When we hit our puberty, our opinion changes. This change will occur as per the environment and society you are in. These changes affect your thoughts, and you get your own opinion on things as discussed before.

Now, our parents have always used to guide us from the beginning. We listen to them, follow them and live. But now at this age contradictions will start. Because your parent's era was far more different from the present time. Just look around yourself and see there are so many new things that didn't exist before. Pubs, clubs, spas, parties, nights out, advanced technology, connectivity, and so much more. They were not before, but they all come by time. As our parents are not really aware of them and they find it hard to understand the new trends that are very common for new ages, they find it contradictory to their traditional lifestyle.

And now here comes what we all call restrictions. We always complain that I am restricted by my parents from doing this, doing that, and more. These restrictions occur because of the change in day-to-day life of beings. And here parents mostly want their kids to get far from these things and live life the way they eyed it because that's right as per them. And let me tell you, they are not wrong, because changes take time.

Now you will find it very hard to make your parents admit it because you are a **COOL KID OF THIS TIME**, and you want to do new things. That's how human nature is; we all want to try new things that attract us. And clubbing, parties, and traveling are some of them. Club programs offer a new enjoyment to us with dance, food, and fun that we all want, which attracts us.

And do you think that this will be done alone? NO.

Of course not. This all requires a bunch of people around you whom we call **FRIENDS**.

Going to functions and parties with your friend gives you a sudden joy and enjoyment that you feel from inside. But why? Why do you feel happy with them?

Well, when you spend time with someone and you both share your thoughts and opinions, and if they match, then you become friends. And of course, there is no doubt that being with people with our mentality will give us a sense of enjoyment and completeness.

Why do we need friends?

Why do we need them? What do they give us? Can't I live alone? I don't need friends? These can be the questions that you might be having in your mind or have heard people saying them. Well, a person needs friends to get what they want too. Friendship is not just a relationship, but it's an attraction and a connection that you make yourself.

From the birth, we have got so many relations as son, brother, uncle, nephew, and more. But that one relation that you make yourself is friendship. Friends are the emotion that makes you feel existing. That's how I define friendship.

A friend is not only the one who is with you in fun moments, but it's also one who gives you a shoulder to cry on. The most famous quote: **"Everyone will be with you in your happiness, but the one who takes your side when you are sad and alone is a friend"**.

When you are feeling down because of any reason, it can be because of your personal life, professional life, or any other problem; you sit stressed and just worry. But just think how good and wonderful it will be if you can just speak out all what you feel; this will reduce your stress and worries.

Yes, it really does. Do you know why you cry? It is because when you are so filled with your secrets and things that you cannot speak out with your mouth, then your eyes take the initiative to let those words drop in the form of tears.

So, it is really important to speak out for yourself. When you speak your thoughts out loud and get a supportive response from that person who understands you, then you will get the power to fight with your situation and get the courage to win.

Why Not Our Parents?

Because of the difference in your opinion and their opinion. I already discussed before how the difference is created in thinking with time. In such a situation, you will think 100 times before sharing anything with your family.

How will they react? What will they answer? Will they understand me? Will they support me? What if they beat me? And so many more questions that you get into your mind when you think about sharing something with your parents, and they are all common. We all get such questions because what if instead of support we get scolded?

But when it comes to sharing all of your dead listed things, your sins, your curses, you share them very happily and openly with your friends because of the sense of comfort they provide you. You know very well that this person understands me, and if I tell him/her something, he/she will just tell me do's and don'ts. Or sometimes, they just beat you because some of your flaws are so big that you get a kick or punch. But still, that fight and those comfort zones that we get from our friends are unconditional, that we love and we want.

Innocent Lie

How many times have you lied about going to study at a friend's home and then you both went outside for fun?

How much money did you and your friend save or even steal to top up in your favorite game?

How many times did you say you had a project to do, but instead you were dancing in a club with your studious friends?

Well, well, we all did these things, and many of us still do. Listen, life is not a cage. You have to enjoy it in the way you want. And I am not saying that you can steal or murder someone. Nope, not at all. We all have different perspectives about our pleasure. Some of us like to sit in a peaceful place while some want to rock all day and night with loud music. That's all your choice . Do as you want, just do not to do something that can backfire on you and can create a big issue ahead.

I am a very open-minded person. And my friends even used to drink and smoke. But I never touched those things. And my friend is still a totally drunker. So, what happened was there was a party with full alcohol support, and so friends drank 3 to 4 bottles. And now he is the best politician, philosopher, and a person with truly so dense knowledge that you can never think of. That's how drunk people are. And yes, you know what? They are such a good dancer too. The one who had never stepped onto the stage before was literally jumping and dancing like Shakira. I was like, "I don't know this person," until he shouted my name loudly to invite me to dance there. Now in front of all people, I have been invited by the drunk person who is roaming like a shake over the stage—what could be the best action? How about just shutting your mouth and going away?

But yes, I am a friend. So, I took him off the stage and kicked him out to his home.

Isn't this wonderful that the one who gave you a shoulder to cry on is now being kicked like a dog? Well, that's the beauty of friendship, right?

My Story: From Shadow to Light

We all are not lucky enough to get all those cool things and good friends like I discussed above. They are mostly shown in movies and dramas, and some lucky people get to feel that in reality.

I am also one of those unlucky ones, or I consider myself lucky. I will tell you my story first, then let's discuss later whether I was right and wrong.

I used to be a very friendly and open person. Back in the 2020s, I had a very close friend, or he was actually my best friend. We used to study in the same school and also used to go to the same tuition classes. And he also came to my home to play games most of the time.

This all looks beautiful, right?

But to be honest, it was not so. I am personally an addictive person. If I have someone with me and he is my best friend, then I am very greedy; my bestie is only mine, not of others. And that's where we always lacked because my bestie was used to being with others as well, sitting with others as well, partying with others too, and so much more. And I used to be very jealous of all these things all the time. I asked him about these and told him how I felt about all that. And also, that you are my best friend. I actually always felt that I was the one who was forcing things upon him. I feel so bad about how I forced him to be with me. I actually asked him so many times to stay with me, but the situation was the same, and as we used to spend time together, I got attached to him.

Time goes by, and COVID came. Our school was closed, and our meetings as well. I had his number but didn't dare to text or call. That was the time I hit my first depression. Yes, at the age of 15, I got my first depressive phase, which lasted for 3 months. I got clearly blank, and I did not talk to my family. I used to do nothing but just sit with no emotion and expression for hours. I am literally telling this; the people who are in depression are literally fighting the toughest war with themselves. And it was not someone else's fault. It was me. I got addicted to him and think of him, and lately I've been alone and in depression.

Know why?

I will briefly explain the solution to this, but after another story.

I love to explore things and meet new people. Personally, I am very interested and passionate about learning new cultures, traditions, and festivals and about people from different countries. It always excites me to learn from the local people of that country, so I got online foreign friends. At a time, I met and talked to so many people at a time, like wow, from Indonesia to South Korea, Japan to Spain, the USA to Europe, Russia to Thailand, and Australia to Brazil, so much. I had a lot of people on my Instagram handle with whom I used to talk a lot and have fun. It was actually the end of 2022 and early 2023. The COVID situation was also calm. I started to go to school, but I always waited for the school bell to ring so I could go back home and chat with my friends.

But suddenly there came a very deep silence within them all. The phone, which used to buzz all the time with notification sounds, was like on silent. The pop-up is not coming anymore, and a sudden funeral came across my social media account.

Just think of a person who used to chat most of the time with so many people, who actually had 10+ social media applications to connect with different people, the one who took a bite of food and stopped to reply to the message, the one who used to say that he was going outside for a walk and then used to call for a long time and talk, the person who gave all his time, attention, efforts, and everything to be with people around him and even 10,000 km away with all his honesty and dedication, is now waiting for that one buzz sound again.

I know that many of us did this and at last have been like me, "SILENT.". When you hear nothing from your surroundings. When you not get that much support that you used to give to others, when you are left alone in completing the other people's needs, when you don't recognize what you feel and what you want because you are busy in completing things of others, what do you think that what you are doing with yourself? Yes, you are pushing yourself back into depression, and this way I hit my another depression, which lasted for 2 months, was actually worse than before.

Crying at night, hiding from yourself, going out for a walk alone, showing a smile when you accidentally find someone, laying down with no desire to learn or do anything, just want to stay in very deep peace. That's what a depressed person looks like. My mind was completely out of thoughts and all shit and ideas I had been thinking about. **I tried to cry silently by covering my mouth with my hand and feel the pain in my throat of the loud shout that wanted to come out so badly**. I had no friend till that time. Online ones disappeared, and offline ones were busy in their own things. And I, I was left like a stupid. It's very hard to describe the feelings and empty emotions of that period. I had been fighting with myself. I was feeling like I was lost in dark space. And I was not able to find a way to get out of it. The more I try, the more I get stuck in it, so I stop trying anymore and wait, wait, wait until I heal myself. The process took a lot of time, but finally I came out of it.

Let us now see what were the 5 wrong decisions and actions I did that put me into that situation. I want you to read them carefully so that you don't do wrong things that I did.

Firstly: I made so many efforts to be what others like.

I changed myself for my best friend so that he can just be with me. That was my mistake. **"Never change yourself for anyone. The person who wants to be with you will be with you with whatever personality you have, by hook or by crook. He/she will never ask for any change within you because the one who accepts you will also accept your habits, your personality, your do's, your don'ts, and your soul"**. So, I request to all of my readers that they never charge themselves for anyone. **Everything in this world comes for a specific period of time to perform a specific task or to teach us something meaningful**. So why change yourself for some bunch of people who will be with you for some time?

Secondly: I lost myself in the race of a being like others.

This is much related to the first, but it is different. When I was trying to make myself get into a particular group of my friends, I didn't know that they even considered me as a friend or not; I pushed down my own thoughts and opinions and said 'Yes' and 'True.' I even agreed on matters that, factually, were not really liked by me. I suppressed my opinions and thoughts, which was the beginning of losing myself because I was being a puppet who could be controlled by anyone. I got to realize this so much later and want to say to all of you that you **should raise your voice when you don't agree**. Don't act like a timid cat who is always looking around for approval. If you feel different, if you think differently, then don't be scared or afraid to share your opinion. Say it, and if they accept it, then it's very good. And if they do not get out of there.

You know why I lost attention from other people because I lost my self-respect and my humor within all of them. And when a person does not have self-respect and humor is not more than a toy to others. They just use it when they are bored and throw it away after a while because it has no value. **Never lose your value. Your value is in your hands**.

Third: I Rejected Myself

Yes, I made myself feel that I cannot be happy by staying alone. I made myself so busy for a time that I don't have much more to do or to do what I actually want to. I made myself surrounded by so many people that I had started to enjoy that fake happiness as my true joy. I neglected what my hobbies were and what I was passionate about. And when suddenly all of them were gone, I had no time to rescue myself from falling down and crying out. I admit completely that it was my fault. Of course, I was the one who did all this, but I don't want you to do anything like this with yourself. **So never try to hide what you actually like**. Because when you do what makes you actually joyous from inside, that defines your true worth. But if you just keep going and hanging out with people who don't care about you then, I let you estimate your worth yourself.

Fourth :I Was Crowded

You can see how I got shifted. First my bestie was a source of joy and happiness for me, but later on, when I got depression, my perspectives got charged, and I started to find happiness in a group of people. I was so busy replying to this, that, those, etc. Never do that, please. It was actually my stupidity that I did that. **You should never overcrowd yourself. Be with a limited number of people who are actually important to you and make you feel true and real. The fewer people you have, the more you are connected with yourself.**

Fifth : I Was Not Alone

Spending time with friends is important. Going outside for a hangout and chill is important. Chilling and having fun is also important because we are humans. We have got a life and a beautiful world to enjoy by ourselves. **"But in this world of sparkly things and shining stars, we should not forget ourselves"**. Try to spend some time with yourself only.

Just take a pause from Instagram, Snapchat, Facebook, Tinder, Twitter, and WhatsApp. Just stop them for some time in your day and sit calmly and relax.

Take a deep breath and think about yourself.

What's your goal?

What do you need?

What makes you happy?

who you are?

What is the purpose of our life?

Why are we alive?

What is your own worth?

These questions come to all people at some specific age, can come before puberty or after puberty. No wonder in that; the wonder is how many times you tried to find the answer to them. We all do the same things; whenever we get such questions into our minds, we just divert our minds either by watching Netflix and eating popcorn or doing any other unnecessary stuff. But try once to find the answer to these questions, and you will know your worth and your importance. The leaders we have now, like Tim Cook, Steve Jobs, Bill Gates, Elon Musk, and Jeff Bezos, were not the ones who ignored these questions. They dove inside themselves, gave themselves some time to find answers, and built a better version of themselves that we all can see now. **Be persistent, take your time and do your work; the rest of the things will work on their own.**

What if someone doesn't want friends?

Well, I have said this thing that everyone is different. What is right for you is not necessarily right for everyone. OK?

And you cannot force someone to be your friend. Friendship is a connection of hearts with no brains. Yes, that's true. With your friend, you act so stupid and totally do nonsense. You and your friends can be serious as well, but mostly we call them idiots.

Ok, let's be serious now: friendship is a very deep inner connection of two hearts where you both share your thoughts and ideas and find comfort or feel good by being around them.

But what if someone's heart is not open? He/she doesn't want to get surrounded by people? Yes, it does happen. I have personally met so many people who don't like to have friends because they enjoy themselves. They have found a fulfillment and completeness within themselves that they don't want it to get interrupted by someone else. So, they just don't allow people to enter into their lives.

Or the other reason can be like the story I shared before; I can say that I was strong enough to face the situation and rise up. I have built a better version of myself. I don't have many friends now, and I limit myself with my feelings and emotions. I put barriers so that if someone leaves me, then I will not be crying or sad again. I limited my own feelings so no one can come close to me, and also I stopped sharing everything with others, but some people who go through the same or even worse situation that I had faced are not strong enough to rise up and trust everybody again.

It leaves a very long and lasting impact on them, which they find very hard to believe and trust someone else again. So, they also build a new version of themselves in which they just be with themselves and try to find their own peace and harmony.

The Incomplete-Completeness

What happens sometimes is you are surrounded by many people and enjoying all together. You do everything that you want, but at the end of the day, you find that something is left to do. or I may say you have forgotten something?

How many of you like to go to meetups and be with friends?

How many of you are with your friend but still feel uncomfortable or not truly happy?

There are many moments where we have to be present because of our responsibility, and we wear a very good mask of happiness on our face and go there. We act like we are having all the fun, right? You did that too? Oh, you did. Well, I also did it multiple times, so don't worry about that.

There is actually a quote that is like, **"You choose for yourself"**.

I will explain it more, so don't worry. You are the owner of your life and everything that you want for yourself. You make things for yourself. You earn for yourself, and you spend for yourself. Don't you?

So why do you find it so hard to choose people around you with whom you want to be and want to get rid of? Is it that much harder? Or you are just a lazy fellow?

When you don't feel the real joy from inside and when you are surrounded by people or friends, but at that time you just want to leave from there or you feel insecure at that time, then let me tell you one thing: that's not the place for you; that's not what you actually deserve. So, it is better to leave that site better than haunting there. You have to find yourself with what type of people personality you like to be with and on what subject you like to talk about. If you once make an effort to find it, then it will be very easy for you to be actually jolly, and then you will live your true life with yourself without friends or with friends.

With this, we have come to the end of this chapter. At last, I will tell my dear readers to try to find your true place. Friendship can be as beautiful as a dandelion flower, but for others it can also be as a bare field. But for both of them

"Friendship can pave your path to your goal but cannot be your ultimate destination. Work on yourself . Find yourself and rise up yourself".

Chapter 6

Online Friendship

They are fake?. It doesn't last long. It is useless. They don't care. It is just for 1 month. You guys can never meet. Video calls and chats are not enough and so on.

These are the statements that we all hear so much about when it comes to the most fascinating and growing term, "online friendship." But are all these statements that are mentioned above actually true? Is online friendship or online friends so problematic?

Does it really happen that they just use you like a toy and throw you away after they are bored? Firstly, I am not a monk. I also use social media and had seen so many videos and posts about this topic. Some say truth, and some just say rubbish. Social media and the Internet are the platforms where anyone can post anything. It can be the ultimate truth, or it can also be the imaginary situation or someone's own perception. So, what is your work to do?

Your work is to analyze what is shown to you and then come to acceptance or rejection. You have a brain, not a landfill, where you put everything that is not of your need. Keep it clean and precise.

What is this online friendship?

A very simple and easy definition for all who are not aware of this term can be "**When two people meet on any social media application through the Internet and share their ideas and thoughts and tie up in a relation called friendship, it is known as online friendship.**" In this rapid growth of the Internet and connectivity, we all are becoming more and more inquisitive. We want to know about our surroundings, but more, we are excited to go overseas and find out something new by which we can relate ourselves.

We all have so numerous software and so many more applications that are available on our smartphones, and we can easily spend our whole day with them. Wondering how? Netflix, or it can be chatting? right? Exactly yes! You got it!!

Rapid replies! Different emojis so many gifs! Cute stickers! Hilarious jokes! and a good friend who can spend a whole day with you on mobile chat. Tap - Tap Well, well, I have already discussed friendship, so I won't be explaining it here again.

But what if you don't have any friends to chat with? Then we have got so many applications where you can find someone to chat with. These are called friendship apps or also termed as language exchange applications.

It goes very smoothly; you just have to sign up, type your interest, and then you will get a list of all those people who match your interest, like on your tips. Just send them and start chatting; that's all. Very easy, right?

What happens next?

When you actually start chatting with a person, and you have some time, then you both try to show your best side to each other, mostly we start our conversation with "Sup!". You both start chatting and introducing yourselves, like, "How are things going?" All your attention and focus are on that mobile device and replying to that person. You both talk about your hobbies, likes, dislikes, and more. That's how it starts. On the first day you will feel warmth in your heart, and it will grow little by little.

What actually happens is when you meet a new person, your brain cells activate and try to capture every minute detail about that person and store it. In real life, when you actually meet someone. The first you see is their clothes and look. I am not a racist, and I do not discriminate on any basis. But it is actually true that when you see someone new, your brain will create a first impression based on the person's style and looks.

But in online friendships, you just see some pictures that are posted on profiles and talk to them. So, in this situation, you try to figure out the person's personality, attitude, way of talking, and gestures by just that chat. And you both show your best to each other, and it's natural so that you both get a good image of yourself in each other's mind.

A beautiful illusion

Now that you both have presented a very good image of yourselves to each other, you have built a strong connection between the two of you.

When two people are talking to each other without any disturbance and all their senses are focused on just that reply, then every word that comes out matters, and that's how you also reply very consciously.

After having such a long conversation with a person whom you met just a few hours ago, you are now not chatting because of some work you got. What do you think will be happening in your brain?

Our brain is very naughty. It always tries to find relaxation and do easy things so that you can chill. And while chatting with that online friend, you had a very beautiful time because you had nothing much to do but just reply and relax. You were all in it, and by that you considered that time as a happy moment for you. What you actually miss is the presence of that person and their replies because they gave you happiness, which now you need, and your mind directs you towards it.

You will not find anything good to do, no doubt, for the next few hours. Once you stop chatting with that person, you will find ways to get free and start chatting again. And this will happen for sure.

And when, after some hours, you come back and start talking to that person again, you find an ultimate happiness within that moment because you were thinking about it all the time and now you finally got it. This will actually continue with you for at least one week. You miss, then you are back, and you are happy again. You will find a sense of completeness when you are actually with that person, and when you are not, you think something is missing around you. But is it correct? How does it affect? How does it affect your real-life friendship and other things? Let's see →

Running off from reality

Yes, you actually run off from the reality. And it happens to all of us, but we barely notice. When you keep on putting efforts into the same person for days, then your desire increases, and you try to spend more and more time that you can. And you try to make time from your schedule. Instead of spending the time with your real-life friends, you give that time to your online ones. You change your schedules for that person, and so more you do because that person created a good importance in your life. And if you are getting the same hard work back from your friend, you get wings to fly high.

The downfall

Everything comes to an end after a specific period of time. What you see as beautiful is not necessarily beautiful in real life or from the inside. Everyone has its goods and bads. After so many days where you have been taken care of so nicely and talked a lot. You both shared everything and also shared every secret because of the sense of comfort that you had felt during that period of chatting. But things don't really last beautifully always. Do you think that you will always be able to show your only best side only to others? No! You cannot. You can hide your true self for some time, but at last you come out of yourself. That's how it goes.

After spending so many days together and talking day and night, your actual behavior starts to come out. Slowly but surely. And you cannot control it. The way you talk and show yourself can change on what you are mostly all the time. And this is where many friendships, sorry, online friendships, come to fall down, because after being portrayed like the wisest and perfect person, now you see the reality, which sticks into your mind, which is hard to accept. Because of that, you get a little sort in your chats. But this can not only be one reason.

Another reason is: You are not the only one. There are so many people on these applications, and the one who wants to chat is not so into you. If you both talk for some hours and then you get some peace of work to do, then do you think that he will be waiting for you holding that mobile and singing like Cinderella? No, dear, no! It's not a fairy tale, so wake up. That person will just get another one like you to talk to. And if the other one is more interesting and freer than you, then sadly, you are no longer in the chat list to reply quickly and within seconds because you have been displaced.

Priority List

This is actually something that I personally believe. We all maintain a priority list within ourselves. Who is on top, and who is at the bottom? It's all upon us.

Let me give you a very simple example to relate with.

Tik-Tik Notification from your classmate. (You can ignore it or reply later if you're busy.)

Tik-Tik Notification from your loved one (Leave everything and you reply that first)

Why?

Why did that happen that you just ignored the message from your classmate or a friend, but when it comes to your lover or best friend, you just stop everything and reply first? Why?

We all do this, and we barely think about it. The reason is: **Priority List**. We maintain a sequence of people who make us feel good, happy, and are important to us. We put them on the top. And people who mostly talk nonsense and waste your time come at the last of the list.

It can vary from person to person; some put their family always on top, and as teenagers, there are some contradictions with thoughts and understandings because of what teenagers put their friends on top of who match their vibes. And if you are in any relationship, then your lover is on top.

Is online friendship really fake?

We cannot conclude something by just our thoughts and what we think is right. Everything works well but sometimes it works badly too. It just depends on the person. So far we have discussed online friendship, or LDF (long-distance friendships). You might be having a very vivid image of LDF as a breaking, disheartening, and short-term timepass friendship. But actually, it's not like that.

Right now, I have 2 online friends with whom I have been together for over an year. I gave them the nickname Kitty and Princess. One is from Poland and another one is from Russia. We never met before; we just texted, called sometimes, or even barely, and that's how it went, so what was before that we discussed?

Well, that was just one side, and now we will be discussing the other side of LDF.

Listen, LDF is not about doing hours of chat, calling every day, sending beautiful images, and sharing every shit you did today. No! It is not like that. It is about sharing your concern, helping when the other one feels sad or down, standing by your side when no one is there, and also making fun of each other.

There are many moments when your online friend can support you more than your real life friends can. It is also a matter of time that when you need your friend. Maybe your real one is busy, but you get a supportive hand from your online one. And also, sometimes we develop a better understanding with online friends and mutual connections that makes us feel even more comfortable, and it does not finish just in some months or years. But besides all this, don't completely forget your real one and your responsibility.

"Time and conditions can vary and make things look different to you, so it's better to have patience and understand the situation".

You will never be able to know the real essence of friendship if you start counting the number of days you met, how many places you visited together, and more. Look, everyone has their own things to do. No one is free. So, stop thinking or imagining that someone will come into your life who will text you 24/7 and do all the stuff like picnics, hiking, the beach, parties, clubs, etc. These things are all shown in dramas & movies and have created a strong impression on ourselves that we conclude our fun in only these things. Come to reality: if you have time, it doesn't mean that your bunch of friends also do.

If you just share one beautiful or heartbreaking time of your day with your LDF or real-life friend, it is far more impactful than your 1000 messages a day. If you just stay when your friend is actually in a situation where he/she needs someone by his/her side, then it is far more beautiful than going to any beach or any club. And if you can just call your friend even once in a month to just spend some time and share some moments, then it is more precious than 5 to 10 hours of calls a day.

Either your friend is online or offline; it's your responsibility to take care of the relations that you make yourself. Don't expect anything from others because you will be left crying at the end if you do expect something. Just do your part well, and that's all.

"A beautiful friendship is like a diamond in the jewelry of your life. It takes time,

effort, and patience so it can shine for a
long time".

?.

Chapter 7

A Remarkable Journey of Love

It may sound very beautiful and very painful, depending on the past experiences. We all have given various definitions to love as per our need and forgotten what the real meaning of love is and how it actually feels. We all have made ourselves feel every attachment is love, and we start manifesting things and become daydreams.

I am not going to give you any more or some definition of love again because you guys will forget it in a few days. We all already have so much stuff inside our head that putting something more to it will just be a blast. I will just try to explain the real meaning of love and how far we have changed it.

How we actually made new connections and named them as love.

Why can't we differentiate between love and affection and end up by taking the wrong decision?

Why is it actually hard to accept love?

How did we make ourselves blind in this world of lightness?

And so much I want to tell and discuss with you all, so let's start simply and easily.

LOVE

This word of four letters plays a very significant role in everyone's life. Love is not something you can buy with money. If you think you can, then I know what you are thinking: that money can buy everything. But no, dear, the inner satisfaction you will never be able to get with money. There are so many billionaires who actually get divorced. They had so much money, but still they ended up getting divorced. So, one thing we can conclude is that money will not be the way to love. Love is actually an emotion and a feeling that comes from the inner soul within you, and it just happens once. It is not like it will happen multiple times. No, it's not. Love is a one-time emotion and feeling that you get for a very special person who cherished you with something that you have been craving for.

The word love can have different meanings from person to person. We define love by ourselves, but we actually forget the core of it and end up with conflicts. The best example I can give to all of you about love is given by Buddha, which is:

"When you like a flower, you pluck it, but when you love a flower, you water it every day."

That is actually the real beauty and feeling of love.

"When you like someone, you get attracted towards that person and want to be with that person, but when you love someone, you be with that person without caring

about the future consequences and how long it will take".

Affection vs. Love

Heard these two words a lot? Right, but did you ever try to understand the real meaning, difference, and application of them in your real life?

We all come through affection at some time, but as we don't really know about it, we neglect it.

Let's take a short real-life example so we all can relate to it.

Think that you got a new classmate in your class who is really beautiful and charming; your eyes are on her, and you want to talk to that person desperately. As soon as you both start to talk and spend time with each other, you both get to know each other more well. Then you feel an attraction towards each other and want to be really close. After all this time, you both have already talked that much that after a few days you don't have anything new to say to each other and now you are silent. Next you meet someone else and get interested in her and forget about the past one.

What do you guys think it was? Was it really love that lasted for just a week?

We mostly consider it as love, and then we start to weave new dreams of togetherness, dates, and more and more. But as soon as you wake up and you find that the person is now gone, you feel bad for some time, but again you start looking for love.

Guys, it was actually affection. Love and affection look very familiar and are even hard to figure out. In affection, you actually want to get everything as quickly as possible, but **another name for love is patience**. Love is not something that can happen to someone within a day or minutes. No! Love takes time to identify, appreciate, conclude, and then to accept.

We often make mistakes here. Affection is a short-term feeling, while love is everlasting.

As you saw in the previous example, how things went so quickly and everything was set to be called love, but at last just one thing broke it all.

"Love is never breakable. It is one of the finest jewels that is enlightened for years and years."

How to Identify

Take your time and let things work themselves out. I am a great believer in myself. I believe that what is meant for me will reach me under any consequences. That is why I do not rush to achieve something. I just do my piece of work and relax. That is how I have been going on. If you are attracted to someone, then first you do have to know about that person. Knowing is the first step. If you are very quick to things and want to make up in just 10 to 15 days, then it's pure affection.

For love, give each other time, understand each other, know about likes and dislikes, explore, and do it really make you feel different among all; can you wait for that person for your whole life? Question yourself and try to get the answer.

I am telling you that the soul within you can never give you a wrong answer, but just the thing is that you have to hear it clearly and accept the truth. People also say that they do everything in love and affection. But time tells everything. The one in love will be loyal even if his/her partner is 10,000 km away. But the affectionate one will start flirting with others even when his/her partner is 10 mins away.

You have to conclude yourself by time, efforts, honesty, and reality.

How do we define love now?

Time continues, generation changes, thinking changes, and meaning changes. That's exactly what happened to love. In today's time, love is just like a fun thing. Love means hookups, parties, clubs, bars, spending money, going on dates, and exposing each other to everyone that you two are together and do so many things so far.

It does actually sound like an entertainment movie, but that's how people consider love now. And all these meanings of what we discussed right now contradict the first and another name of love that we discussed, which is Patience. We don't have time and patience. We all are in so much of a hurry to get everything and enjoy it in exactly the same way we did with love. Today we meet, tomorrow we talk, after 2 days we come into a relationship, after five days we start conflicting, and then on the seventh day, we break up. In this time period we do everything that year's old couples do.

One more thing I want to discuss and tell you all is that. I said we expose ourselves. How do you think we will define this?

Expose

In some days of meeting and chatting, we start sharing our pictures.

First, cute ones, and in love actually, we get a desire to see our loved one if he/she is not close to us. But there is a time when we start opening our clothes in the name of love. It is actually very common nowadays, and we all have successfully given another name to love, which is "bed.".

Is it really? Like, is love something that is short and out of emotions?

Firstly, let me tell all of you that if ever your partner asks you to open your clothes in the name of love just in 1 or 2 months of dating, then stop there. A person who is in love will protect you and make you feel safe and comfortable. In the starting months of dating, you guys don't even know each other well, but getting an invitation to do things takes so much time.

You are not a sex worker or a toy who is here to complete the sexual needs of someone. If you don't feel comfortable, stand for your decision. Because in love both of the partners agree on something to conclude. If any one of them is not feeling comfortable or thinks something is wrong, then what's the point of continuing it? If you are being forced to accept the decision that has already been taken out of your choice then do you still want to be part of such a relationship?

"Love is not about being physical with each other. It is about being a part of others internal peace".

Your partner will think 100 times before doing something that makes you feel uncomfortable and unsafe. And he/she will always respect your opinion and decision. Because you are his/her responsibility now, of whom he/she has to take care.

How does a person feel when in love?

I am not going to create any new fantasy story that says a person in love always dances like a butterfly; he/she always smiles, and lovely music rings in his/her head. No, that's all meaningless. You are not having a radio in your head that plays music.

A person who is in love is just like others. The way he reads and talks to other people and his behavior remains the same as before. He is also a human, so we all are common. Just one thing that changes is his attitude toward his partner. Just that. Being more concerned and careful about things, situations, and making memories, dreaming to be together, and making future plans for both of them.

It sounds very beautiful but takes a very long journey in which they both have to walk together. Just these changes occur within lovers. A lover does have a responsibility, which he takes on himself to make his loved one comfortable and happy. A beautiful life doesn't mean that the couple will never be having a hard time. Life is a roller coaster ride. There will be times when you both will be having a hard time; all you have to do is that: deal with it patiently. A conflict can last for a year, but if you want, you can make it end in minutes. Because your partner is more important than all those meaningless arguments. I have seen many people who broke up, and their relationship was not just of short time period. Some of them lived together for years together, but at some point they had a conflict, and no one had that much courage to sit with the other one and discuss it. We make our own assumptions and reach our own conclusion, which is, in reality, far from real conditions and consequences.

When a conflict arises in a relationship, three stories are created:

1. **The story one partner understood.**

2. **The story the other partner understood.**

3. **The story that could have resolved everything if they had sat together and discussed it, allowing both to understand.**

Be mad with each other for some time; it's fine, and if you don't want to talk to the other one than just stay silent for some time, but please don't let it keep on going for long." **Silence can be the answer to many questions, but it can also create many misconceptions".** Reach out and talk and be happy together.

Be supportive to each other and be with each other. Half of the problem solves itself when you have someone by your side to support. And the rest will be solved by discussion and a positive approach.

Conflicts: A turning point

We all have fights. Either it is with our loved one or our most loved enemy. There are various points where our thoughts and ideas don't really match with others, and at such moments when any one of the people is not stepping back, no one can stop from having a conflict.

There are fights in love life too. Some are small and cute ones, but some are actually not. Listen, if you ever get into a fight with your loved one, then just try to ignore that situation and say sorry, and why? Because by saying sorry, you can end up a big conflict from happening. Your value and self-respect will not go down. Don't worry.

The one to whom you are saying sorry is none other your loved one. He/she is very well aware of your behavior, attitudes, goods, bads, and everything stupid you did as well, then by just a word, sorry, it will not harm your self-esteem. It is just a simple word. It is not necessary to say sorry only when you are wrong, but you can also say sorry when someone is actually more important to you than just these 5 alphabetic words.

I would like to add something here: please be understanding to each other because it is very necessary. If someone is always saying sorry, then it's not like you are always right. Try to put yourself into your partner's situation and then make a decision. If you are disappointed by something or mad at something, then tell them and consult about it and make it sorted. **"Because sometimes, even the smallest spark can ignite a fire capable of consuming the entire forest".** I hope you understand.

You can't reset things!

You don't have the time machine of Doraemon by which you can go back into the past to make things better if you ruin them now.

"Think before you speak!". We always listen to this, but have you ever tried it out?

Whatever you speak makes an impact on the listener. It can be good and bad depending upon you. Just be careful when you are talking to someone because when we are angry, we say every shit out of our mouth, which can make someone else feel insulted or bad. Even if it's your best friend or BFF, there will be some point where that person feels bad but wouldn't actually say it because you also mean something to that one, especially if it comes to introverted people.

It is your responsibility to take things in your hand and lead them. Don't take it as a burden but as a responsibility, ok?

So, promise me now that you will always think before you speak and be using more positive words.

To Those Who Lost Someone Precious

I know the exact feeling of it. I am also like you all and have been in a relationship, and I don't want to explain much about it. It is very hard to control yourself when you come to this moment. Because of whatever reason you had, it doesn't matter. Even if you are wrong or right. Just the actual thing that matters is that you gave yourself to someone else to handle all your emotions, happiness, feelings, and desires and made a dream to always be the same way when you both were together.

Have you heard the song "Angel Baby" by Troye Sivan? I really love this song personally because of the way Troye defined the actual beauty when you are with your loved one and want to stay like that forever.

You don't know what the future and destiny hold, but you just want to enjoy that moment for long. That moment becomes a memory later, and you wish to have more like it in the future.

When someone likes and then leaves you, it looks like you lost yourself because you already gave all of yourself, and now you are left barehanded. I don't say that this is your mistake. No! I just say that LOVE has got beauty and pain together. It can heal your wounds but can also give you scars when it comes to an end.

When you actually cry alone, you can't stop thinking of your lover; you regret your own decisions and feel guilt; you find it very hard to continue, especially at night. Night is the time when, after doing all of our day stuff, we finally go to our bed to relax. All the things and memories go in reverse through your brain and break you down. For a heartbroken person, night is the toughest time, and even more so when he is alone. Because when you are alone, you wouldn't be able to hold yourself. All those beautiful times have now become memories; all those promises are broken; the sense of completeness is now gone, and you are just like this, and you want to cry out loud.

I wouldn't say to you not to cry. I always recommend to people that if they have a very hard time and want to cry, then just cry. There is nothing to be ashamed of. We all are the same, and we all have a tough time. If smiling and enjoying good times is fine, then why is crying at hard moments something to be ashamed of? When you cry loudly without any worry of being heard by someone, then you throw out all your frustration and stress. The tears drop one by one; our eyes turn red, our hands just want to hug ourselves, and your legs don't really support you to stand anymore. The loud voice, which was kept quiet by you for a long time, finally comes out as condolence, which is of yourself because you actually did not lose your precious one. But actually, you lost yourself, and now you are left with nothing.

Have you guys got very much pain in your throat while crying? Why did you let your opinion and let your voice down when they actually needed to be raised up? Just to keep a person with you? Or you are just not confident in yourself about what you have to speak? Or you are just a coward? If you could have spoken out at the time when you actually had to, then it wouldn't have been like this. Please speak whatever you feel. Never let the inner voice inside you quiet because it is always right and is for your good. Never beg someone to stay with you. I told this before as well, that if someone is going to stay with you, then that person will. But if someone doesn't, then you will be pointed out for every small mistake and doing.

You are very precious, dear. Take care of yourself.

Why do they cheat?

I will give a very straightforward answer to this question: just one answer, nothing more.

When They Are Not Satisfied by You

When someone is not actually satisfied by you, it means that you don't fit into their demand and need. Yes, demand, that's correct. It can be anything: you are not pretty, not handsome, tall, short, poor, rich, stylish, intelligent, dumb, or anything. There are multiple reasons to hate someone, but if you just focus on any one quality to love someone, then you will be with that person for life. No need to praise every time; no need to lie; just say what you feel and keep that one quality in your head all the time.

And also, if your partner, fortunately or unfortunately, gets hit by someone more beautiful or cool than what you are, and their feelings just shift from you to that person because humans are greedy organisms. A human's desire and greed will never end. And he wants all the beautiful things to be kept around him. So that's how it goes.

One solution or an idea that I think is necessary in partners is to be loyal to each other.

If your lover really loves you from all his soul and heart, then you will be his last place to rest. Understand?

And he may see other people around, but you will always be the most gorgeous and beautiful to him. If I am in any relationship, then for me, my partner is the most beautiful, pretty, and lovely person among the crowd.

Can love happen again?

I will be honest. I consider love as a one-time feeling. As I already discussed, love is an emotion which you get from one special person. And you can't change that person with someone because you are bored or want to try something new. If you love a person, then you made a commitment, and you have to stick to it.

I already told you the difference between love and affection and also that love takes time but affection does not. So, you should wait for the right one. I have seen people who had 5 on 6 relationships, but now they are still single. The reason was very simple. Before knowing each other well and developing a better understanding, they get into a relationship that ends up with conflicts or differences.

I would also like to mention that the affection brings sadness while love brings sorrow, which is lifelong. You will never be able to replace it. Never and ever.

Not always close

It's not necessary that you and your loved one will always be together. It doesn't happen. And this even gets harder when you have a long-distance relationship when people meet each other online and fall in love (not affection; I am talking about actual love, which takes time) and then get in a relationship, which embarks a new journey for them. LDR itself has a beauty of patience, video calls, messages, sharing feeds, and making you not feel alone even if someone is 10,000 km away from you. Such loved ones have to wait for the right time and have to work hard to make their dreams come true. It requires efforts and belief in one another rather than blaming the situation and crying over it that you are very far away. Stop doing that. Don't blame others and the scenario for your condition because you made it yourself. If you think you can make it and you believe in your partner, then don't care about anything that comes into your way and just promise to fight with everything together because **"Cheap products are easily available, while expensive ones take time to find".** Cherish every moment and make a beautiful future together.

?

Chapter 8

When did we lose ourselves?

How many times have you found yourself confused with your own thoughts?

When you actually wanted to do something that you were really passionate about, but because of some reasons, you put your thoughts and ambitions down.

It happens to everyone at some point; sometimes we have to put ourselves down to keep things going with the flow. But what if you always have to be down? Why is it that you always bow down to your morals, your desires, your dreams, and your ambitions because of a particular set of people or something else that is getting in your way?

Well, I am also one of you all. I am well aware of the restrictions and rules that we all have to follow. But there is something I want to share with all of you.

Yes, it's my personal experience, so actually, I was also used to doing the things that make others happy and make me shine. The works and tasks that I did in my past were actually out of my hobbies and desire, but still I did a lot for some limited praise. During that I was happy for that particular moment, but after that I got my way changed. I truly learned numerous lessons from time till now. And I got a change in myself that I stopped doing things that made me shine in their point of view. Rather, I started to discover myself. I started to do what I always wanted to and kept on going with that.

Believe me, I didn't get happy but got joy, which was not actually for 2 to 5 days but everlasting. If right now I remember those moments when I did all what I wanted without worrying about how others think about me, it still makes me feel very comfortable and awesome. If I could do that, then why can't you?

Can't we all just forget about what is going on around us? Can't we take a pause from our well-planned and busy lifestyle and think just about ourselves, that is, am I really happy with all that? Can't we just do something that makes not others happy but makes ourselves feel our existence and feel delighted?

I wish I could make other people do so. To just take all other burdens and throw them away and give them a day to live. But actually, I can't, and neither can any of us do so with others. No one is coming to find you within yourself. You have to do it yourself, dear. Just try and feel that moment, OK?

Society

"We live in a society where a good deed earns praise from 10 people, but a small mistake invites blame from 1,000". Your one unusual act, which is not normal for you, will make them forget all your social work and start to criticize you till death. I feel bad for those innocent ones who were scolded, threatened, intimidated, and deterred when they tried to do something on their own for themselves without caring about their surroundings. So, let's just do something for ourselves without caring about what others say. If you made yourself the one who does not care about others opinions, then you will always live happily.

Be Greedy

Sometimes it's better to just get your own space in the crowd. Did you get what I actually meant? I mean that sometimes it's better to worry about only yourself. Yes, exactly! greedy! Be greedy for yourself, be greedy for your dreams, and be greedy for your choice. It's not wrong. If you are greedy for your own joy and you don't care about other things going on around you, then you are the happiest person. Let others talk about you. Let them say good or bad or anything they want to. Does it harm you? Will their words give you scars all over your body, or will they kill you? No, nothing happens in real life. We just think about those comments and feel bad and not do something like which made people say that. Are you also one of those who gets in their bed after all day and then feels bad, like that particular person said I looked ugly in a black dress, so will you just stop wearing it? People who want to poke their nose in someone else's business will do it anyway. It will not be only you there but 100 more whom that person gave a harsh comment. This doesn't mean you just stop doing something. Just go ahead with your own choice and do what makes you feel great.

How many times have you changed yourself?

So, count yourself that how many times you have changed your way to walk, way to talk, how you eat, dress, live, personality, behavior, and even you got yourself into something that is truly very far from you.

Why did we do that, dear?

The two most expected answers can be because of love or friendship.

Do love and friendship really require changes? Changes of personality and your behavior?

Well, the answer is NO for both of them. If you are charging yourself for someone else's need or to make others happy to make them stay with you, then this is your worst decision. Never ever change your true self for anybody. No one has that much privilege to ask you to charge the way you are. No one got that right. If someone ever asks you to do so, then just say, "Thank you for being with me; I hope you will have a bright future ahead." That's all. Love and friendship are those jewels of this world that don't require any change.

They are acceptable to your true self. Your true friend, your true love, will accept the way you are. It doesn't matter if it's very different from others'. Everyone has something special that makes them different among all. But if you are turning that special identity of yours to turn into a normal person, then you will be missed among the crowd.

Just take an example that some of your friends don't like your nose; then will you change it? Even if you do so for that friend. He/she will point out something new to get off from you. "**The one who needs to go has to go**!" You can't stop someone for staying by your side. Nor are you a robot who can modify itself as per need. So, what could be a better choice? Then why don't you just stay as you are? Be happy with yourself. If one person is going than you will be meeting 10 more in the future, but if you lose yourself, you never get it back.

"Embrace your own light, the right ones will find you in its glow, but if you let it dim, even you may lose your way."

?.

Chapter 9

Burden Of Societal Ethics That Restricts Gen-Z

Let's first learn about Gen Z. Gen-Z, also known as Generation Z, refers to the generation of those people who were born in between 1997 and 2012. We divide generations to better understand the culture, social, and impact of the individual. This also helps us to keep track of technology and advancement, which will be basic resources that will be provided to those who are born in these generations. Like all of my readers who are reading my book, they will be of Gen-Z.

The change in generations leads to the change in the thinking, opportunity, relation, culture, and many more, which will be different from our parent's generation. Things that we are seeing around are pretty normal to us, but they were not at the time of our parents, which makes it hard and long to make them understand something new. Also, the change in mindset often leads to contradictions of thoughts and conflicts as well. To encounter this, we have to be better speakers, and our parents need to be better listeners. But it doesn't really go well easily. There are many societal ethics that are actually forced on us to follow by our parents and society. And it's really hard to convince them and make them understand our own goals and ideology. It actually happens to everyone at some point, and it's not really easy to deal with them. Gen-Z, which is growing up with the internet, social media, and smartphones, is actually very smart and strong. Gen-Z is very adaptable to changes, which gives them the ability to handle the situation and problems in a better way, but when it comes to dealing with our own parents and the society, it is really hard.

Let's see the ethics of society which are actually restrictions in the growth of Gen-Z:

Rigid Career Expectation

How many of you were told by your parents to be a doctor or engineer? I can guarantee you that at some point your parents have surely mentioned that they want you to be a doctor or engineer or even a lawyer sometimes. Because these jobs are paid well, and as per our elders, money = success. If you are in any of these occupations or any other and you were paid well, then you will be considered successful. If you don't have money, you are not successful.

While it's completely opposite in Gen Z. Mostly, Gen Z actually does not focus on the money first, but they focus on their passion. They prioritize their creativity and work-life balance rather than working 24/7 and earning money. Success to them does not actually mean a bank account that is full of money, but the real success to them is when they work and enjoy doing it. They like to work for their passion and then earn. Money is needed to survive, but there are various ways to earn it. Choosing the traditional career path is not the option for Gen-Z, but exploring their own interests and working on it to earn is their goal.

Unrealistic Standards for Success

Do you remember how our grandparents used to say that, in their time, people got married at 12 or 13? Even today, this still happens in some places like Rajasthan, Bihar, Assam, and Telangana. Thanks to government efforts, more people are aware now, but sadly, these cases still happen every year.
On top of that, society still expects us to follow certain timelines. By 23, you should have a good job. By 27, you should get married. By 30, you should have kids and settle down. These ideas have been passed down for generations, and even now, parents and relatives start to pressure us and also tells us about this and that person and society will start gossiping if we don't follow them. It can be frustrating, especially when times have changed, but these old expectations haven't.

First of all, let's be honest—those who gossip are usually the ones who have nothing better to do. They don't have much going on in their own lives, because if one is busy in their life, then that person will not be having time to discuss their neighbor's affairs, because he will just give time to sort his family and own problems first. So, they find entertainment in peeking into others' lives. They love to discuss how many kids someone has, where the family goes, who they talk to, who visits their house, and so much more. They put a surprising amount of dedication into this work and if they could have put the same number of efforts on other work than they would have been better.

Gen-Z sets their own standards, goals, and commitments. They don't live by old timelines that have been passed down for generations. For them, achieving their goals and fulfilling their dreams often comes first, and marriage is secondary—or sometimes not even on the list. Many of them don't see marriage as a necessity and choose to stay single because they don't want to share their life with someone else and also don't find themselves ready to take on the responsibility of their partner as well. And this is a better option than having conflicts in the future.

And for those who do consider marriage, love marriages are often preferred over arranged ones. Spending your life with someone you truly love and connect with feels much easier than suddenly committing to a stranger as your lifelong partner.

Resistance to Changing Norms

The idea that men should work and earn money for the family while women stay at home to take care of the kids has been a deeply rooted belief in our country for ages. Along with this comes the notion that women shouldn't step out alone, that they always need someone to accompany them, and that men should be treated better simply because they are the bread makers of the home. These outdated ideas continue to hold back gender equality, a cause that women are still fighting for. The question remains: how much longer will it take to break free from these restrictions?

Gen-Z is doing a great job when it comes to gender equality. They believe in giving everyone the freedom to choose. Going out, having a career, and enjoying a balanced life is normal for them. For most Gen-Z, the main goal is to be financially independent so they don't have to depend on anyone.

Whether it's a girl or a boy, freedom and choice should belong to the individual. If someone wants to work outside, support them—don't trap them within four walls.

Another important factor is accepting change. A simple example is the LGBTQIA+ community. People in this community still face many hardships in gaining equality. Many have to hide their true identity and pretend to live like others because their preferences are seen as different. They are often labeled as unnatural, treated unfairly and also ignored by society.

To make it clear, being part of the LGBTQIA+ community is completely natural. The person standing in front of you isn't the only one—about 7% of the world's population belongs to the LGBTQIA+ community. When so many people share the same identity, it's evident that it's natural. Sexual orientation is a normal variation of human biology that develops before birth. People don't choose their sexual orientation. It's simply a part of who they are, just like heterosexuality is for others. No one chooses their sexuality—we are all born with it, and it's something that we should accept. And it's not something that just appeared over time. Homosexuality has existed throughout history, but society's narrow rules and judgments kept many from speaking out about it. In the past, many people had to hide their true selves because they feared rejection or punishment. But now, more people are embracing who they are and accepting what they were born with.

We should respect everyone's choices and preferences. If we can't, we have no right to judge or comment on anyone. Gen-Z is leading the way in being more inclusive and accepting. They embrace who they are without shame, whether they are homosexual or heterosexual, and they accept the changes happening around them too.

Hustle Culture and Overworking

We are often told to focus solely on our studies, and while this advice has merit, it reflects a narrow perspective. Older generations tend to equate achievement with education alone. If you spend all day and night studying and overwork yourself to the point of burnout, it's often seen as a badge of honor. But what about balance? You're not encouraged to focus on sports or hobbies for long—these are merely "pastimes" to them.

The main goal, we're told, is to find a stable job. This mindset sees sports as a mere hobby, not a viable career. Interestingly, while they expect athletes representing the country to bring home medals, most parents would never want their own children to pursue sports as a profession. Take cricket, for example, the most popular sport in our country. Playing cricket is seen as normal, even celebrated, but if you choose to pursue a sport other than cricket, people begin to question you. This bias holds us back.

We fail to encourage young athletes, often disregarding their efforts because they're not earning immediately. And yet, when the Olympics come around, we wonder why our country doesn't win enough medals. Can we really ask that question? How often have we introduced our children or siblings to new sports outside of cricket? How many times have we praised someone playing a sport that isn't cricket? Look at Neeraj Chopra. When he won a medal, the entire country got in celebration. But what's changed since then? Are we doing more to nurture talent in diverse sports? Are we finding and fostering the sport's most suitable for each of us? Unfortunately, we are stuck in outdated habits and traditions, and our lack of consistent support for sports continues to hinder us.

If we want to see true progress, we need to reflect on these questions and work toward creating a society that values and invests in all forms of talent—whether academic or athletic.

That's what Gen Z focuses on. Maintaining a work-life balance is a key aspect of living in today's world. Don't just work like a donkey—working hard is important, but working smart is the true game-changer. Gen Z is becoming increasingly aware, not just of local opportunities but also of global trends. This awareness provides them with the ability to explore what they are good at and choose the best path for themselves.

Education will always be the foundation, but a traditional 9-to-5 job is no longer the only option for this generation. With the growing prominence of the sports industry, many young people aspire to be part of the sports revolution. This movement has the potential to produce enthusiastic and hardworking athletes who can bring medals home and elevate the country's status in global sports. However, this shift will not happen on its own. It requires collective effort and collaboration.

To achieve this, schools and governments need to work together to encourage sports from an early age. By introducing a variety of sports—both indoor and outdoor—as well as online gaming, we can ensure holistic physical and mental development for young individuals. This early exposure will allow children to discover their interests and talents, helping them make informed career choices in the future.

Online gaming also has a great future ahead. International events and tournaments happening around the world are providing opportunities for new gamers to take the lead. IN 2024, an e-gaming tournament in Saudi Arabia became a massive success, even surpassing traditional indoor and outdoor sports in terms of impact. Over 200 gaming clubs and 1,500 players participated, with 500 million viewers and a prize pool of $60 million.

So, we shouldn't punish or make fun of someone for pursuing a career in gaming. Instead, we should support them. The key is balancing studies with gaming and making informed career decisions based on individual passion and strengths.

It's time to break free from conventional paths and embrace diverse opportunities. Together, we can create an environment where the youth can thrive, excel, and contribute meaningfully to society.

Conformity Over Individuality

We are all introduced to our culture and traditions from a young age. Seeing our surroundings and celebrating festivals together helps us learn about our ancient traditions. Our elders put a lot of emphasis on maintaining traditions, often believing that things should continue the way they have always been. They are usually not open to changes in society, which can lead to conflicts.

One clear example of this is the criticism of self-expression. When you wear something different from what's considered usual or traditional, you may become the center of attention. People might stare at you or question your choice of clothing, especially if it's not considered 'normal' or in line with their traditions. You'll often have to listen to these comments and judgments from others.

I want to question to the questioners that: why do you have to mind other's business. If someone is wearing what is not really usual to you than, you could just ignore it, What's the point of passing your negative comment on someone, if you can't give some positive complements? It's the choice of the person how he/she wants to get dressed. Let them do whatever they want to you do what you want. That's all.

Gen-Z, which is exposed to global fashion and traditions, has a broader perspective when it comes to fashion and self-styling. I'm not saying you should forget your own culture—you should always have knowledge about where you come from. But after that, you can choose for yourself. Modern fashion and dressing styles are very different from traditional ones, and it can be hard for those who aren't familiar with it to accept.

Long and unique hairstyles, fashionable clothes, and accessories are all part of this style. Gen-Z focuses on individuality, which makes their looks different and unique from others. It's about rejecting rigid societal norms and embracing individuality in self-expression—whether that's wearing accessories, dyeing your hair bold colors, getting tattoos, or exploring other artistic forms. The priority is to balance conformity with personal uniqueness. Be what makes you feel confident and unique.

Reluctance toward mental health awareness

'Men don't cry.' Heard this a lot, right? This statement is mostly used to show the strong and tough behavior of a man. I want to ask, why? Why can't a man cry? Isn't he human? Doesn't he have emotions and feelings? Or is there something wrong with his eyes that can't shed tears? So why can't a man cry? And it's not just this one. There are so many quotes used for both men and women to make them hide their emotions and feelings.

For years, we weren't aware of mental health problems. Does that mean these problems only started recently? No, they have always been with us, and as time has passed, they've continued to increase. The issue is that we have limited our thinking to the point that we don't want to address them.
We often treat mental health issues as temporary problems that will go away on their own, but that's not how it works. These problems can leave a lasting impact on a person's life, affecting them long-term. They are often seen as signs of weakness or failure rather than legitimate health concerns. That's why people tend to hide their struggles instead of talking about them when they need support. These issues have always been

present, but we were never taught about them. We study everything from history to technology, but we don't learn about mental health, how to deal with it, or how to support others who are suffering. This lack of education contributes to the many suicide cases, where a person feels isolated and overwhelmed. The tragic reality is that no one knew what was going on, because they kept it to themselves. Why? Because society hasn't created an environment where people can freely talk about mental health issues like depression, anxiety, panic attacks, and more. We fail to provide the education and awareness that's needed. We are harming our future by not addressing these issues openly.

I have already mentioned before that when a person is experiencing depression and other mental health problems, he or she is fighting a war within themselves. That person is fighting with culture, friends, family, tradition, their own thoughts, desires, aims, and so much more. Do you think it will be an easy war? This is really tough. And when it does happen, the impact is felt in our daily lives as well. Our behavior changes towards everyone. And the most ironic thing I know is that when a person's behavior changes, the family thinks that the person has been given the evil eye or has been jinxed. Then, they take you to a priest, where he blows on your head and performs some rituals. Like, really? Do you even know what that person is suffering from? Instead of taking them to a consulting psychologist, you are performing rituals over that person. It's not going to solve the problem but will actually make it worse because of such behavior from the family members.

Gen-Z is not far from it. They will be facing a lot more mental health problems because of the sharp difference between the culture they are living in and what they want. It will be very hard to deal with it alone. Solving everything on your own is not always the best solution. Sometimes, we need to speak out and ask for help from someone so we can receive proper guidance. Talking to someone who understands mental health problems is really necessary in this age. They are there to listen to us and help us. It does happen that our elders do not understand us, and that's fine. Seek out a psychologist, share everything that's on your mind, and listen to them.

"Taking care of your mind is just as important as taking care of your body because both deserve to heal and thrive"

Respect is one sided

We must respect our elders. Respecting elders is not only a part of every culture but also our moral duty as responsible citizens. We give them respect because they are older than us, more experienced, and have learned valuable life lessons that they can teach us. However, in our culture, we often experience that respect is regarded as one-sided, meaning only elders deserve respect. This mindset leads to a widening gap between elders and Gen-Z youth.

Our culture places a strong emphasis on hierarchical relationships, which are based on levels and ranks. For example, the grandfather, then the father, and then you. Elders often feel responsible for maintaining discipline and take on the authority to correct the younger generation. They aim to pass on the same traditional values they received from their fathers, hoping that the younger generation will live a well-disciplined life.

But nowadays, it often leads to a negative approach and arguments between parents and the younger generation. If you are constantly told that fire is hot, you will remember that it is hot, but you will surely touch it one day to see if it is really true or not. And when you feel the warmth of it, you will realize that it is truly warm and dangerous as well. What you learn from fire is a lesson you learn yourself. The lessons you learn on your own are lifelong in your mind, and you will always remember them more vividly than the guidance given by elders or parents.

Having a different opinion and presenting it is often regarded as disrespectful by our elders. When you share what you feel about any topic, and if it's not what they want to hear, it will be considered that you are not following their path and guidance, making you a "bad kid." That's what I am. I am a "bad kid" to my parents because I don't listen to them. My thoughts and perceptions are much different from theirs, which creates a gap between us.

In our puberty, we go through changes that are quite common. These changes vary depending on the circle and environment in which you live. Gen-Z tends to embrace innovation and diversity. They prioritize independence and personal choice in areas such as career paths, relationships, and lifestyle decisions, which are completely opposite to the traditional norms that have been followed for years. These changes may be perceived as a lack of respect for family values and as disrupting the traditional economy.

Our elders often take pride in resilience and sacrifices, and they expect the younger generation to uphold these same values. Meanwhile, Gen-Z prioritizes well-being and work-life balance over traditional family responsibilities, which is often seen as disrespectful. Elders find it difficult to understand the behavior and lifestyle changes of the younger generation, which are shaped by globalization and technology.

All these factors make the older generation feel disrespected, which leads to a gap between generations. As a result, elders sometimes become tough and behave harshly towards their younger ones, which has a more negative impact on them. The younger generation feels that their opinions, emotions, and challenges are not taken seriously, which creates an imbalance in the relationship.

The younger generation wants acceptance for their opinions, while elders view this as disrespect. To overcome this, a respectful conversation and better understanding from both sides are necessary.

 Elders need to understand and respect the opinions of the younger generation, giving them the opportunity to explore and learn for themselves, rather than just listening. Meanwhile, Gen-Z should remain calm, be helpful toward elders, and respect their opinions as well.

Chapter 10

End Of Era

Getting through changes and fighting with different ideas and thoughts is very hard. We have to make ourselves stable and keep on going because if we fall down once, then we will be left behind. So, you have to keep on going instead of sitting down and waiting for the situation to turn out well. We make our destiny ourselves. If you are just believing in your faith and not doing your hard work, then you will be getting nothing. Even when you have a hard time, you have to rise up for yourself. The challenges that I have explained before are the most common ones that we all face at some point. After walking through all these, we learn lessons and try to build some better and meaningful connections ahead. Learning is an everlasting process. We never stop to learn. The one who takes a lesson from every situation is the one who is a step ahead of others. Teenage years don't just teach us about the meaning of relationships and help us find our true selves, but they also prepare us for the challenging world ahead. It marks the beginning of creating our place among others.

I started to notice the situation changes from the age of 15, and by the time I turned 18, I had encountered many inspirational people who really helped me. Not only in academics, but they also became my personal guides when I needed them.

School Life

After entering school, we all make a lot of friends and get to know each other better. We play together, take part in competitions, compete in exams, and celebrate together. But during this journey, we form crucial friendships that don't just end when we leave school. These are the ones with whom we may not talk often, but whenever we do, the energy and excitement remain the same as before. This is because of the pure connection we have built with each other.

I didn't have a very big group of friends because I'm not great at handling a lot of relationships, so I cherished a few close ones instead. I fondly gave them nicknames that reflected their personalities: Mr. Bean, Witch, Raavan, Gol Gappa, Mr. Serious and Doll. Each of them played a significant role in my life, and I am grateful for the unforgettable memories we created together. They were far more than just friends; we were emotional, mental, and academic guides for each other.

The Farewell

It was truly a sad moment for all of us. When we conclude our school life, the last function we celebrate is our farewell. It's a goodbye ceremony organized by our juniors to honor the time we spent in school. In this moment, you see faces you may have never noticed in class before—whether it's the one who has been scolded all year or the one who won all the awards. You find each of them there because this is the only time we gather together to celebrate with our teachers and friends.

We take countless pictures, share stories, and reminisce about every moment we have lived in this school. We enjoy performances by our juniors, and at the end, we cry. The attachment to coming to school daily, chatting with friends and classmates, learning from our teachers, and the environment our school provided—all of this hits us at once, making us emotional. Even if you have always hated your school, you will find sadness in leaving it behind.

We all face such moments where we have to leave our past and happiness behind to take steps ahead for a brighter future.

Embracing the Future

As we step into this new chapter, we carry with us the lessons learned, the friendships forged, and the memories created. The world outside may seem daunting, filled with uncertainties and challenges, but it is also a canvas waiting for us to paint our dreams upon.

Remember, the end of one era is merely the beginning of another. Embrace the changes, for they are the stepping stones to your growth. Each experience, whether joyful or painful, shapes who you are and who you will become.

As you venture into the unknown, hold onto the values you've cultivated: resilience, empathy, and the courage to be yourself. Surround yourself with those who uplift you, challenge you, and inspire you to reach for the stars.

In the end, life is not just about the destination but the journey itself. So, take a deep breath, step forward, and let your story unfold. The world is waiting for you, and it's time to make your mark.

ACKNOWLEDGEMENT

First and foremost, I would like to thank myself for being strong and resilient. I have learned to rise after every fall, to wipe away my tears in moments of solitude, and to be my own source of support when no one else was there. This book shares my journey and the hardships I faced, revealing that these struggles are universal, yet few have dared to document them in a way that could help others. I took the initiative to write about the challenges and changes we all experience in a smooth, easy, and relatable manner.

I also want to express my gratitude to my MPSM Grace Convent School family. They provided not only an education but also a nurturing environment that helped develop my personality and embrace my true self. Without their support, I would not have had the courage to pursue my skills and hobbies.

I will continue to write and strive to be a source of support for those who seek it a place where you can rest your head and find relatability in my words.

Late Dr. Myera Singh

To my late principal ma'am, **Late Dr. Myera Singh**, whose presence left behind a light of enlightenment for many to follow. A lady of remarkable strength, vision, and unwavering will, she devoted her life to the betterment of her students. Her dedication was not just to academics but to building lives. She believed in improving the quality of education and making it a joyful journey rather than a burden. She served as the cornerstone of **MPSM Grace Convent School, Mathura**, shaping not only the institution but the hearts and minds within it.

Every word she spoke carried power and encouragement. Her teachings extended far beyond textbooks — they were about life, values, courage, and self-respect. She taught us to fight with dignity and to pursue success with integrity and hard work.

"Don't be in the crowd, be a leader," she would often say — a line that still echoes in my mind and continues to guide me. She is the one from whom I learned to develop my skills, embrace my hobbies alongside education, and remain persistent in my pursuits. I would not have been able to publish this book without the guidance and belief she instilled in me from the very beginning.

Her admiration for us and her tireless efforts left behind a legacy — a foundation upon which many lives like mine have been built. She taught us the value of discipline, focus, character, and leadership.

My every book will include her as the star shining bright in the sky, leading me on my path, lighting up the way whenever I falter. Thank you, ma'am, for being our strength, our guiding light, and the source of so many dreams. We are forever indebted to your love, belief, and unwavering presence in our hearts.

About The Author

Aman is a 19-year-old aspiring author currently pursuing a Bachelor's degree in Engineering. With a passion for exploring and writing about the real-life challenges that many face but seldom discuss, Aman aims to shed light on the complexities of adolescence through his debut book, *Moments We Couldn't Speak.*

As a new writer, Aman draws from his own experiences navigating the beautiful yet challenging landscape of teenage life. He shares the gaps and helplessness he encountered during his formative years, hoping to provide guidance and support to others who may be struggling with similar issues.

Aman's writing is characterized by relatable scenarios, valuable life lessons, and motivational conversations that resonate with young readers. He believes that by opening up about these common struggles, he can help others feel less alone in their journeys. He can be reached at - aman.chaudhary9210@ gmail.com